A Time to Speak
and a Time to Listen

100 poems
selected by
Celia Warren

Schofield&Sims

First published in 2013

Editor: ***Celia Warren***

Celia Warren has asserted her moral right under the Copyright, Designs and Patents Act, 1988, to be identified as the compiler of this work.

Previously unpublished poems, appearing in print for the first time in this anthology, are as follows:

Poem 11 'The Ghosts of Weeds' by Nick Toczek
Poem 45 'Jacks' by Jan Dean
Poem 51 'Taking a Chance' by Roger Stevens
Poem 59 'The Kiss' by Sue Hardy-Dawson
Poem 74 'The Note' by Jill Townsend
Poem 76 'Needle and Thread' by Celia Warren
Poem 77 'My Sock and an Old English Proverb' by Celia Warren
Poem 79 'Shirts for us Kids' by Gerard Benson

British Library Catalogue in Publication Data:
A catalogue record for this book is available from the British Library

Commissioning by ***Carolyn Richardson Publishing Services*** *(www.publiserve.co.uk)*
Design by ***Oxford Designers & Illustrators***
Printed in the UK by ***Charlesworth Press****, Wakefield*

Paperback ISBN 978 07217 1205 5
Hardback ISBN 978 07217 1225 3

For Ray

A time to love

You came and looked over to see what I drew.
The pictures don't matter – my pencil drew you.

Foreword

There's a poem in this book that I first heard when I was very small. It is Poem 97 'Nod' by Walter de la Mare. My mother used to read it to me, from an anthology she had won as a school prize. Many years later, when she was very old and losing her memory, I read it to her and she joined in. That poem had stayed with her when nearly everything else was gone. After she died I asked a friend to read it at her funeral.

Coming across 'Nod' was like meeting an old friend. There are other old friends here, some of whom I first got to know at primary school. I've always liked Poem 72 'Cargoes' by John Masefield – and Poem 96 'When a Knight Won his Spurs' by Jan Struther, which we used to sing in assembly.

Then there are poems that I got to know and love when I was older. Edward Thomas is one of my favourite poets, so I was glad to find three by him: Poem 6 'Lights Out', Poem 18 'Thaw' and Poem 99 'Adlestrop'. Charles Causley is another favourite – read Poem 27 'What has Happened to Lulu?' and Poem 57 'Good Morning, Mr Croco-doco-dile' to see if you agree. Perhaps the two most famous poems in the book are Poem 43 'Daffodils' by William Wordsworth and the sonnet beginning *Shall I compare thee to a summer's day?* by William Shakespeare, presented here as Poem 87 'Eighteenth Sonnet'. I know both of those by heart, so I can take them with me everywhere.

As well as the old friends, there are poems I didn't know and poets whose names are new to me. Some of these may well become favourites as I explore the book and re-read the ones I like best. But I don't expect to like everything. There may be some poems in this book that don't appeal to you. If so, don't give up on poetry. Look for the ones you like and read them again and again. They may well become friends for life.

Wendy Cope

Contents

Note for teachers

A **Teacher's Guide** is available to accompany this anthology. Providing introductory notes on every poem, and poem-specific guidelines for reading them aloud, this practical handbook helps teachers to use the anthology as a basis for speaking and listening activities. The **Teacher's Guide** also gives suggestions for school assemblies that draw upon the rich resources of the anthology for exploring issues such as social awareness, personal growth, families, friendship, responsibility, self-confidence, decision-making and the environment. For further details, please see the back cover of this book or visit **www.schofieldandsims.co.uk**

Introduction

Time is a strange thing. It flies when you are happy or busy, and crawls when you are not. People advise you not to waste it. You try to save it. You want to make good use of it – but how? 'There is a time for everything', says the writer of Ecclesiastes, at the beginning of the lines that inspired this collection of poems.

Some of the poems are serious and will make you stop and think. Others are descriptive and paint pictures for you to share. A number are humorous and will make you laugh. Some are sad, and will comfort you when you feel sad. All are worth reading more than once – and you may find yourself learning your favourites by heart. All explore further the themes touched upon by those inspirational verses from Ecclesiastes, which you can read in the **Prologue** (page 1, opposite).

There is something special about poems that makes you want to read them aloud, or hear them spoken. Most of what you read tells you something – stories, instructions and most of your other reading matter fall into this category. However, poems do more than that. They sing to you, too. They have 'cadence', which is a musical quality of rhythm and tone, and often they include rhymes that please the ear.

As you explore this book, I hope that you will want to read the poems aloud – to yourself, or to friends and family. As you do so, listen to the beautiful sounds of the English language. Allow time to read the poems at your leisure. Don't scan them in haste, as you would a bus timetable. Don't race through them to find out what happens next, as you would a story. Poetry demands time. Take pauses, give yourself space to breathe and reflect. Enjoy this collection to the full, allowing yourself **A Time to Speak and a Time to Listen**.

Celia Warren

A Time for Everything

There is a time for everything
And a season for every activity under heaven.
A time to be born
And a time to die
A time to plant
And a time to pull up
A time to kill
And a time to heal
A time to tear down
And a time to build up
A time to weep
And a time to laugh
A time to mourn
And a time to dance
A time to cast away stones
And a time to gather stones together
A time to embrace
And a time not to embrace
A time to find
And a time to lose
A time to keep
And a time to cast away
A time to tear
And a time to sew
A time to be silent
And a time to speak
A time to love
And a time to hate
A time for war
And a time for peace

Ecclesiastes 3: 2–8

1 Haiku

Avalanche of love
Awakening of angels
A Baby is born

Celia Warren

2 An Elephant is Born

Night holds them safe,
the cloud moon gleams,
deep in the darkness
of soft breath and dreams,
the elephant mother
greets her new son,
with a tender and gentle
low, soft hum,
she strokes his face
the night-left long,
and sings her newborn
elephant song.

Liz Brownlee

3 The Donkey

When fishes flew and forests walked
  And figs grew upon thorn,
Some moment when the moon was blood
  Then surely I was born;

With monstrous head and sickening cry
  And ears like errant wings,
The devil's walking parody
  On all four-footed things.

The tattered outlaw of the earth,
  Of ancient crooked will;
Starve, scourge, deride me: I am dumb,
  I keep my secret still.

Fools! For I also had my hour;
  One far fierce hour and sweet:
There was a shout about my ears,
  And palms before my feet.

G K Chesterton (1874–1936)

4 A Final Appointment

Enter the servant Abdul
His face ashy grey,
Fear in his eyes –
He has seen Death today.

Begs release of his master,
Plans instant flight:
"I must be far from
This city tonight!"

"Why?" asks the Sultan,
A man kind and clever,
"You have said many times
You would serve me for ever."

"Master, I love you,
That much you must know,
But down in the city
A half hour ago

Death himself was out walking,
Reached cold hands to me:
The threat was quite plain
For the whole world to see.

I must leave Death behind!
To Baghdad I'll take flight.
Master, give me a horse –
I can be there tonight!"

So Abdul escapes,
Fear driving him on,
And very soon after
His servant has gone

The Sultan himself
Walks out in the city,
Walks among cripples
And beggars with pity.

Like Abdul, meets Death
As he walks in that place,
Peers into the folds of his cloak
For his face;

Sees it not; hears a voice
That is cold, clear and dry:
"Look not for my face –
See that and you die."

But the Sultan speaks boldly
Asking Death, "For what cause
Did you threaten this morning
To make Abdul yours?"

Death replied, "To your servant
I issued no threat.
Indeed sir, I knew that
His time was not yet.

This morning your servant
Had nothing to fear;
I was taken aback
To see the man here;

Gave a start of surprise,
Knowing well that I had
An appointment with Abdul
Tonight in Baghdad."

Eric Finney

5 Death be not Proud

Death be not proud, though some have called thee
Mighty and dreadful, for thou art not so,
For, those, whom thou think'st, thou dost overthrow,
Die not, poor Death, nor yet canst thou kill me.
From Rest and Sleep, which but thy pictures be,
Much pleasure, then from thee, much more must flow,
And soonest our best men with thee do go,
Rest of their bones, and souls' delivery.
Thou art slave to fate, chance, kings, and desperate men,
And dost with poison, war, and sickness dwell,
And poppies, or charms can make us sleep as well,
And better than thy stroke; why swell'st thou then?
One short sleep past, we wake eternally,
And Death shall be no more; Death, thou shalt die.

John Donne (1572–1631)

6 Lights Out

I have come to the borders of sleep,
The unfathomable deep
Forest where all must lose
Their way, however straight,
Or winding, soon or late;
They cannot choose.

Many a road and track
That, since the dawn's first crack,
Up to the forest brink,
Deceived the travellers,
Suddenly now blurs,
And in they sink.

Here love ends,
Despair, ambition ends;
All pleasure and all trouble,
Although most sweet or bitter,
Here ends in sleep that is sweeter
Than tasks most noble.

There is not any book
Or face of dearest look
That I would not turn from now
To go into the unknown
I must enter, and leave, alone,
I know not how.

The tall forest towers;
Its cloudy foliage lowers
Ahead, shelf above shelf;
Its silence I hear and obey
That I may lose my way
And myself.

Edward Thomas (1878–1917)

7 The Spell of the Rose

"I mean to build a hall anon,
And shape two turrets there,
And a broad newelled stair,
And a cool well for crystal water;
Yes; I will build a hall anon.
Plant roses love shall feed upon,
And apple trees and pear."

He set to build the manor-hall,
And shaped the turrets there,
And the broad newelled stair,
And the cool well for crystal water;
He built for me that manor-hall,
And planted many trees withal,
But no rose anywhere.

And as he planted never a rose
That bears the flower of love,
Though other flowers throve
A frost-wind moved our souls to sever
Since he had planted never a rose;
And misconceits raised horrid shows,
And agonies came thereof.

"I'll mend these miseries," then said I,
And so, at dead of night,
I went and, screened from sight,
That nought should keep our souls in severance,
I set a rose-bush. "This," said I,
"May end divisions dire and wry,
And long-drawn days of blight."

But I was called from earth – yea, called
Before my rose-bush grew;
And would that now I knew
What feels he of the tree I planted,
And whether, after I was called
To be a ghost, he, as of old,
Gave me his heart anew!

Perhaps now blooms that queen of trees
I set but saw not grow,
And he, beside its glow –
Eyes couched of the mis-vision that blurred me –
Ay, there beside that queen of trees
He sees me as I was, though sees
Too late to tell me so!

Thomas Hardy (1840–1928)

8 Plum

Don't be so glum,
plum.

Don't feel beaten.

You were made
to be eaten.

But don't you know
that deep within,
beneath your juicy flesh
and flimsy skin,

you bear a mystery,
you hold a key,

you have the making of
a whole new tree.

Tony Mitton

9 Bulb

Smooth fingers touch my papery skin,
place me in soil
in a shallow hole, cover me.

Loam and grains soothe,
and trickling water comforts.

I rest; seem dead, but only sleep.
I wait.

And all at once, a tingle urges
slender threads to slip from me,
roots to feed me,
roots to anchor me.

And then my head surges
and a shoot, green as a frog,
forces up through earth,
reaches the light.

I shall burst with brilliance,
a blazing trumpet of daffodil
blaring at the sun.

When my yellow fades
to crisp parchment, I shall stay
in my secret cavern, know worm and beetle,
feel my strength return
for next year's flowering.

Alison Chisholm

10 The Nymph Considers the Garden

If you pull all groundsel out of your beds,
hide the towers of plant pots under the shed,
throw out six cracked buckets, the babies' bath,
tie back the tall phlox, whose petals flood paths,
prune purple sage, which invades every lawn,
clear stumps, where the woodpecker cackles at dawn,
you will have a fine plot, tidied and hacked.
Neighbours will love you. I will not come back.

Alison Brackenbury

11 The Ghosts of Weeds

We are the ghosts, the ghosts of weeds
The ghosts of plants which no-one needs
Which negligence, not nurture, breeds.

Yes, we're the ghosts, the ghosts of weeds
Who once were green, who sprang from seeds
But drank the poisoned garden feeds.

Our heads were high, our roots were deep
But now we die on a compost heap.
A bluebell rings and willows weep.
The mayfly sings that life is cheap.

Forget-me-not, for here I sleep,
While, where we grew, long shadows creep
From which it seems as if we peep
With heads held high and roots grown deep.

It's just the ghosts, the ghosts of weeds
The ghosts of plants which no-one needs
Which negligence, not nurture, breeds.

Cos we're the ghosts, the ghosts of weeds
Who once were green, who sprang from seeds
Who drank the poisoned garden feeds …

The ghosts, the ghosts, the ghosts of weeds.

Nick Toczek

12 Good Taste

Travelling, a man met a tiger, so …
He ran. The tiger ran after him
Thinking: How fast I run … But

The road thought: How long I am … Then,
They came to a cliff, yes, the man
Grabbed at an ash root and swung down

Over its edge. Above his knuckles, the tiger.
At the foot of the cliff, its mate. Two mice,
One black, one white, began to gnaw the root.

And by the traveller's head grew one
Juicy strawberry, so … hugging the root
The man reached out and plucked the fruit.

How sweet it tasted!

Christopher Logue (1926–2011)

13 Lovely Mosquito

Lovely mosquito, attacking my arm
As quiet and still as a statue,
Stay right where you are! I'll do you no harm –
I simply desire to pat you.

Just puncture my veins and swallow your fill
For nobody's going to swot you.
Now, lovely mosquito, stay perfectly still –
A SWIPE! and a SPLAT! and I GOT YOU!

Doug MacLeod

14 The Wind

The wind stood up and gave a shout.
He whistled on his fingers and
Kicked the withered leaves about
And thumped the branches with his hand
And said that he'd kill and kill,
And so he will and so he will.

James Stephens (1882–1950)

15 On Killing a Tree

It takes much time to kill a tree,
Not a simple jab of the knife
Will do it. It has grown
Slowly consuming the earth,
Rising out of it, feeding
Upon its crust, absorbing
Years of sunlight, air, water,
And out of its leprous hide
Sprouting leaves.

So hack and chop
But this alone won't do it.
Not so much pain will do it.
The bleeding bark will heal
And from close to the ground
Will rise curled green twigs,
Miniature boughs
Which if unchecked will expand again
To former size.

No,
The root is to be pulled out –
Out of the anchoring earth;
It is to be roped, tied,
And pulled out – snapped out
Or pulled out entirely,
Out from the earth-cave,
And the strength of the tree exposed,
The source, white and wet,
The most sensitive, hidden
For years inside the earth.

Then the matter
Of scorching and choking
In sun and air,
Browning, hardening,
Twisting, withering,

And then it is done.

Gieve Patel

16 The Man he Killed

Had he and I but met
By some old ancient inn,
We should have set us down to wet
Right many a nipperkin!

But ranged as infantry,
And staring face to face,
I shot at him as he at me,
And killed him in his place.

I shot him dead because –
Because he was my foe,
Just so: my foe of course he was;
That's clear enough; although

He thought he'd 'list, perhaps,
Off-hand like – just as I –
Was out of work – had sold his traps –
No other reason why.

Yes; quaint and curious war is!
You shoot a fellow down
You'd treat, if met where any bar is,
Or help to half-a-crown.

Thomas Hardy (1840–1928)

17 Leisure

What is this life if, full of care,
We have no time to stand and stare.

No time to stand beneath the boughs
And stare as long as sheep and cows.

No time to see, when woods we pass,
Where squirrels hide their nuts in grass.

No time to see, in broad daylight,
Streams full of stars, like skies at night.

No time to turn at Beauty's glance,
And watch her feet, how they can dance.

No time to wait till her mouth can
Enrich that smile her eyes began.

A poor life this if, full of care,
We have no time to stand and stare.

W H Davies (1871–1940)

18 Thaw

Over the land freckled with snow half-thawed
The speculating rooks at their nests cawed
And saw from elm-tops, delicate as flower of grass,
What we below could not see, Winter pass.

Edward Thomas (1878–1917)

19 A Carol from Flanders

In Flanders on the Christmas morn
The trenched foemen lay,
The German and the Briton born,
And it was Christmas Day.

The red sun rose on fields accurst,
The gray fog fled away;
But neither cared to fire the first,
For it was Christmas Day!

They called from each to each across
The hideous disarray,
For terrible has been their loss:
"Oh, this is Christmas Day!"

Their rifles all they set aside,
One impulse to obey;
'Twas just the men on either side,
Just men – and Christmas Day.

They dug the graves for all their dead
And over them did pray:
And Englishmen and Germans said:
"How strange a Christmas Day!"

Between the trenches then they met,
Shook hands, and e'en did play
At games on which their hearts were set
On happy Christmas Day.

Not all the emperors and kings,
Financiers and they
Who rule us could prevent these things –
For it was Christmas Day.

Oh ye who read this truthful rime
From Flanders, kneel and say:
God speed the time when every day
Shall be as Christmas Day.

Frederick Niven (1878–1944)

20 Necklace

I had a row with my mum,
stormed off up the stairs,
I really was sorry
to make her worry,
staying out late
without a word.

I tidied my room
and cleaned the shoes,
and made my own packed lunch.
I picked her flowers
and swept the floor
and then I had a hunch.

I could mend her broken necklace,
the one her grandma gave.
I threaded the beads one by one
and counted off the days.

The day we rode on donkeys,
rattling down the beach,
the day she made me chocolate cake
and hid it out of reach,

the day she smoothed my forehead,
when a fever raged within,
the day I held an egg and spoon
and she cheered me on to win.

I gave my mum the necklace,
she wrapped her arms around.
In that delectable moment,
you could not hear a sound.

Chrissie Gittins

21 Demolition Worker

There he is, ten storeys above the street,
Highlighted by his white shirtsleeves,
No hard hat or safety harness
But pick in hand, on top of a narrow peak
Made, not of stone, but of brick.
His way to get from the roof to the ground
Is to knock the building beneath him down,
Like knocking a mountain bit by bit
From underneath your feet
As a means of descending it.
From the way he walks on the wall, pausing to kick
Mortar down with his steel-toed boot,
Everest would seem easy to him.

Stanley Cook (1922–1991)

22 The Spiders Cast their Spell

Break our
web
Break our
Universe

We in return
will bless
you with a curse

May your two legs
grow to be eight

May your sleep be
too light
for the weight
of your dreams

May your house
collapse
at the slight
touch of a breeze

And as you sit
among the ruin
of your memories

May you wish
for thread to spin
May you wish
for thread to spin

John Agard

23 Ozymandias

I met a traveller from an antique land
Who said: Two vast and trunkless legs of stone
Stand in the desert … Near them, on the sand,
Half sunk, a shattered visage lies, whose frown,
And wrinkled lip, and sneer of cold command,
Tell that its sculptor well those passions read
Which yet survive, stamped on these lifeless things,
The hand that mocked them, and the heart that fed:
And on the pedestal these words appear:
'My name is Ozymandias, king of kings:
Look on my works, ye Mighty, and despair!'
Nothing beside remains. Round the decay
Of that colossal wreck, boundless and bare
The lone and level sands stretch far away.

Percy Bysshe Shelley (1792–1822)

24 Spinner

The spider walks across the air
He curls a long foot round his thread
His legs, brown-striped in sunlit grass
Jerk, as wakened from the dead.

So I; at last released from work
Can sit beside the unwashed glass,
See the slow spider stalk through space
Until a green half-hour has passed.

Then, as he twists and firms the thread
There swerves in me this sudden joy
Although his lightness turns a trap
Though all he makes there, will destroy.

Alison Brackenbury

25 Target

Aim higher than the clod of mud,
the thud in earth that's swallowed up,

the belly of a rusted can,
the clang of tin, unbalancing,

snails that cling to low flint walls,
the cracking of a hollow shell,

the plum upon a neighbour's tree,
a hush disturbed within its leaves,

and higher still than startled crows,
slanted attic windows, rows

of chimney stacks, church spires,
tower blocks. Aim higher.

Set sight between the blazing past
and unlit future of a star.

Aim now.

Rachel Rooney

26 The Trouble with Snowmen

"The trouble with snowmen,"
Said my father one year
"They are no sooner made
Than they just disappear.

I'll build you a snowman
And I'll build it to last
Add sand and cement
And then have it cast.

And so every winter,"
He went on to explain
"You shall have a snowman
Be it sunshine or rain."

And that snowman still stands
Though my father is gone
Out there in the garden
Like an unmarked gravestone.

Staring up at the house
Gross and misshapen
As if waiting for something
Bad to happen.

For as the years pass
And I grow older
When summers seem short
And winters colder

The snowmen I envy
As I watch children play
Are the ones that are made
And then fade away.

Roger McGough

27 What has Happened to Lulu?

What has happened to Lulu, mother?
What has happened to Lu?
There's nothing in her bed but an old rag-doll
And by its side a shoe.

Why is her window wide, mother,
The curtain flapping free,
And only a circle on the dusty shelf
Where her money-box used to be?

Why do you turn your head, mother,
And why do the tear-drops fall?
And why do you crumple that note on the fire
And say it is nothing at all?

I woke to voices late last night,
I heard an engine roar.
Why do you tell me the things I heard
Were a dream and nothing more?

I heard somebody cry, mother,
In anger or in pain,
But now I ask you why, mother,
You say it was a gust of rain.

Why do you wander about as though
You don't know what to do?
What has happened to Lulu, mother?
What has happened to Lu?

Charles Causley (1917–2003)

28 The Wind's Prize

Hurling the waves
Twirling the sails
Throwing great handfuls of sand in your face

Flapping umbrellas
Whipping your hair
Lifting the paper and losing your place

The wind searches blindly
For something to snare
A tit-bit to carry off
Into its lair

Suddenly it vanishes
With its new found toys …

A bright yellow lilo and two little boys

Andrea Shavick

29 Samantha is Sobbing

Samantha is sobbing
By the playground wall
But why she should be sobbing
No one knows at all.

The sun shines brightly
The sky is blue
But Samantha is sobbing
Oh what shall we do?

Take her to her Granny
Who lives down Comfort Lane
Once she gets to Granny's house
She'll never sob again.

She'll kiss her on the topknot
And treat her like a queen
Feed her new potatoes
Beans and margarine.

Gareth Owen

30 Daddy Fell into the Pond

Everyone grumbled. The sky was grey.
We had nothing to do and nothing to say.
We were nearing the end of a dismal day.
And there seemed to be nothing beyond,
Then
Daddy fell into the pond!

And everyone's face grew merry and bright,
And Timothy danced for sheer delight.
"Give me the camera, quick, oh quick!
He's crawling out of the duckweed!" Click!

Then the gardener suddenly slapped his knee,
And doubled up, shaking silently,
And the ducks all quacked as if they were daft,
And it sounded as if the old drake laughed.
Oh, there wasn't a thing that didn't respond
When
Daddy fell into the pond!

Alfred Noyes (1880–1958)

Mrs Reece Laughs

Laughter, with us, is no great undertaking,
A sudden wave that breaks and dies in breaking.
Laughter, with Mrs Reece, is much less simple:
It germinates, it spreads, dimple by dimple,
From small beginnings, things of easy girth,
To formidable redundancies of mirth.
Clusters of subterranean chuckles rise
And presently the circles of her eyes
Close into slits, and all the woman heaves
As a great elm with all its mounds of leaves
Wallows before the storm. From hidden sources
A mustering of blind volcanic forces
Takes her and shakes her till she sobs and gapes.
Then all that load of bottled mirth escapes
In one wild crow, a lifting of huge hands,
And creaking stays, a visage that expands
In scarlet ridge and furrow. Thence collapse,
A hanging head, a feeble hand that flaps
An apron-end to stir an air and waft
A steaming face. … And Mrs Reece has laughed.

Martin Armstrong (1882–1974)

32 Laugh and be Merry

Laugh and be merry, remember, better the world with a song,
Better the world with a blow in the teeth of a wrong.
Laugh, for the time is brief, a thread the length of a span.
Laugh and be proud to belong to the old proud pageant of man.

Laugh and be merry: remember, in olden time
God made Heaven and Earth for joy He took in a rhyme,
Made them, and filled them full with the strong red wine of
His mirth
The splendid joy of the stars: the joy of the earth.

So we must laugh and drink from the deep blue cup of the sky,
Join the jubilant song of the great stars sweeping by,
Laugh, and battle, and work, and drink of the wine outpoured
In the dear green earth, the sign of the joy of the Lord.

Laugh and be merry together, like brothers akin,
Guesting awhile in the rooms of a beautiful inn,
Glad till the dancing stops, and the lilt of the music ends.
Laugh till the game is played; and be you merry, my friends.

John Masefield (1878–1967)

33 The Laughter Forecast

Today will be humorous
With some giggly patches,
Scattered outbreaks of chuckling in the south
And smiles spreading from the east later,
Widespread chortling
Increasing to gale-force guffaws towards evening.
The outlook for tomorrow
Is hysterical.

Sue Cowling

34 Pantomime Poem

I'm going to write a pantomime poem
OH NO YOU'RE NOT!
Oh yes I am!
One that will get everyone going
OH NO YOU'RE NOT!
Oh yes I am!

There'll be huge custard pies
And girls who slap thighs,
Men dressed in frocks
And bloomers with dots,
There'll be beanstalks and castles,
Some heroes, some rascals.
There'll be goodies to sing to
And villains BEHIND YOU!
There'll be eggs that are golden,
An actor who's an old 'un!
Cows all called Daisy
And songs that are crazy!

I'm going to write a pantomime poem
OH NO YOU'RE NOT!
Oh yes I am!
One that will get everyone going
OH NO YOU'RE NOT!
Oh yes I am!
OH NO YOU'RE NOT!
Oh yes I am!
OH NO YOU'RE NOT!
I just did!

Coral Rumble

35 Creator

What became of my dinosaurs?
Where did they go?
Carefully crafted
Eons ago.

I gave their colour, size and shape
So much variety.
They filled the rain-washed Earth,
The sky and sea.

The glaciers swelled, the icefields spread
And the swamps grew cold,
Gripping those mighty hearts
In icy hold.

My new creation, furred and feathered,
With warmer blood,
Weathered the melting ice,
Survived the flood.

Now extinction threatens my humpbacked whale,
My rhino and elephant
As my too-successful men
Pillage and hunt.

Maybe, after empty centuries more,
To ease my pain,
I will fill the new-made Earth
With dinosaurs again.

Jane A Russell

36 Dog End Days

Our dog's dead now.

All that's left
are some hairs on the chairs
and a faint doggy smell,
a half-chewed bone, near the telephone,
a fading pawprint, an unopened tin of Chum,
and his lead, hanging hopeless, on a hook.

Our dog's dead now.
All that's left
is a mound in the ground, in the place he liked best
and a strange sort of ache in my chest.

Michaela Morgan

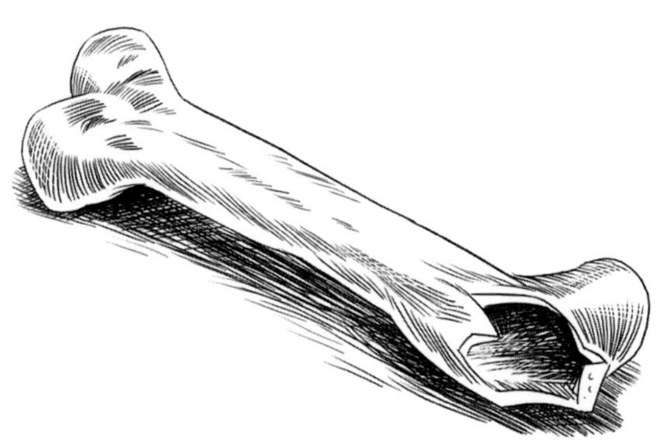

37 Stop All the Clocks

Stop all the clocks, cut off the telephone,
Prevent the dog from barking with a juicy bone,
Silence the pianos and with muffled drum
Bring out the coffin, let the mourners come.

Let aeroplanes circle moaning overhead
Scribbling on the sky the message He Is Dead,
Put crêpe bows round the white necks of the public doves,
Let the traffic policemen wear black cotton gloves.

He was my North, my South, my East and West,
My working week and my Sunday rest,
My noon, my midnight, my talk, my song;
I thought that love would last for ever: I was wrong.

The stars are not wanted now: put out every one;
Pack up the moon and dismantle the sun;
Pour away the ocean and sweep up the wood.
For nothing now can ever come to any good.

W H Auden (1907–1973)

38 When I am Dead, my Dearest

When I am dead, my dearest,
Sing no sad songs for me;
Plant thou no roses at my head,
Nor shady cypress tree:
Be the green grass above me
With showers and dewdrops wet;
And if thou wilt, remember,
And if thou wilt, forget.

I shall not see the shadows,
I shall not feel the rain;
I shall not hear the nightingale
Sing on, as if in pain:
And dreaming through the twilight
That doth not rise nor set,
Haply I may remember,
And haply may forget.

Christina Rossetti (1830–1894)

39 Do not Stand at my Grave and Weep

Do not stand at my grave and weep,
I am not there. I do not sleep.
I am a thousand winds that blow,
I am the diamond glints on snow,
I am the sunlight on ripened grain,
I am the gentle autumn rain.
When you awaken in the morning's hush
I am the swift uplifting rush
Of quiet birds in circling flight.
I am the soft star-shine at night.
Do not stand at my grave and cry;
I am not there. I did not die.

Mary E Frye (1905–2004)

40 Tarantella

Do you remember an Inn,
Miranda?
Do you remember an Inn?
And the tedding and the spreading
Of the straw for a bedding,
And the fleas that tease in the High Pyrenees,
And the wine that tasted of tar?
And the cheers and the jeers of the young muleteers
(Under the vine of the dark veranda)?
Do you remember an Inn, Miranda,
Do you remember an Inn?
And the cheers and the jeers of the young muleteers
Who hadn't got a penny,
And who weren't paying any,
And the hammer at the doors and the Din?
And the Hip! Hop! Hap!
Of the clap
Of the hands to the twirl and the swirl
Of the girl gone chancing,
Glancing,
Dancing,
Backing and advancing,
Snapping of the clapper to the spin
Out and in –
And the Ting, Tong, Tang of the Guitar!
Do you remember an Inn,
Miranda?
Do you remember an Inn?

Never more;
Miranda,
Never more.

Only the high peaks hoar:
And Aragon a torrent at the door.
No sound
In the walls of the Halls where falls
The tread
Of the feet of the dead to the ground
No sound:
But the boom
Of the far Waterfall like Doom.

Hilaire Belloc (1870–1953)

41 The Ballet Teacher

She walks on a bottomless duvet,
her arms carve arcs in the air –

fingers outstretched,
boat-bottom hands,

they fall like feathers
never reaching the ground.

Her circle skirt pleats
glide behind her, beside her,

folding, unfolding –
an opening fan.

Her voice glances each child
with gossamer.

Chrissie Gittins

42 In the Misty, Murky Graveyard

In the misty, murky graveyard
there's a midnight dance,
and in moonlight shaking skeletons
are twirling in a trance.
Linked arm in bony arm
they point and pitch and prance,
down there in the graveyard
at the midnight dance.

In the misty, murky graveyard
there's a midnight rave,
and a score of swaying skeletons
are lurching round a grave.
Their toe bones tip and tap
and their rattling fingers wave,
down there in the graveyard
at the midnight rave.

In the misty, murky graveyard
there's a midnight romp,
and the squad of skinless skeletons
all quiver as they stomp.
To the whistle of the wind
they clink and clank and clomp,
down there in the graveyard
at the midnight romp.

Wes Magee

43 Daffodils

I wandered lonely as a cloud
That floats on high o'er vales and hills,
When all at once I saw a crowd,
A host of golden daffodils;
Beside the lake, beneath the trees,
Fluttering and dancing in the breeze.

Continuous as the stars that shine
And twinkle on the milky way,
They stretched in never-ending line
Along the margin of a bay:
Ten thousand saw I at a glance,
Tossing their heads in sprightly dance.

The waves beside them danced, but they
Out-did the sparkling leaves in glee:
A poet could not but be gay,
In such a jocund company!
I gazed – and gazed – but little thought
What wealth the show to me had brought:

For oft, when on my couch I lie
In vacant or in pensive mood,
They flash upon that inward eye
Which is the bliss of solitude;
And then my heart with pleasure fills,
And dances with the daffodils.

William Wordsworth (1770–1850)

44 Stony

We found this secret beach
Of sea-smooth stones last year:
What fun we had here!
We flung them out to sea at first
Over the running tide,
Your lazy throws
Always the winners
No matter how hard I tried.
Then we bombed blobs
Of seaweed
With nearly fist-sized stones:
At hits and near-misses
Gave cheers or groans,
Till, leaning against two boulders,
Arms round each other's shoulders
We listened to shifting stones
In the tug and suck of the sea;
Last year, you and me.

This year, remembering,
I walked the beach alone
And everything was cold
And grey as stone.

Eric Finney

Jacks

Jacks on a hand back
throw toss turn
come little sister
watch and learn.
Jacks on a slab stone
red rubber ball
bounce in a heartbeat
scoop them all.
Jacks in the shadows
jacks in the sun
silver shine fivestones
the game is won.

Jan Dean

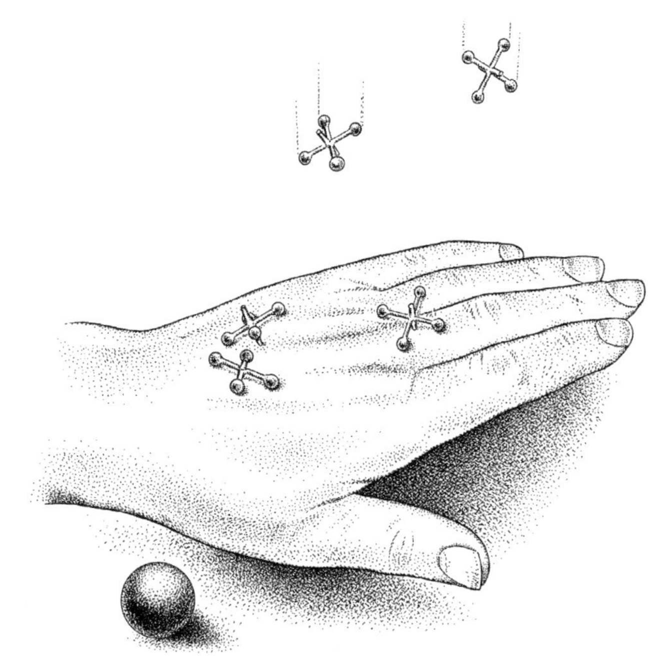

46 The Children and Sir Nameless

Sir Nameless, once of Athelhall, declared:
"These wretched children romping in my park
Trample the herbage till the soil is bared,
And yap and yell from early morn till dark!
Go keep them harnessed to their set routines:
Thank God I've none to hasten my decay;
For green remembrance there are better means
Than offspring, who but wish their sires away."

Sir Nameless of that mansion said anon:
"To be perpetuate for my mightiness
Sculpture must image me when I am gone."
– He forthwith summoned carvers there express
To shape a figure stretching seven-odd feet
(For he was tall) in alabaster stone,
With shield, and crest, and casque, and sword complete:
When done a statelier work was never known.

Three hundred years hied; Church-restorers came,
And, no one of his lineage being traced,
They thought an effigy so large in frame
Best fitted for the floor. There it was placed,
Under the seats for schoolchildren. And they
Kicked out his name, and hobnailed off his nose;
And, as they yawn through sermon-time, they say,
"Who is this old stone man beneath our toes?"

Thomas Hardy (1840–1928)

47 Shells and Stones

Shells and stones on my window-sill
All collected by me.
Shells and stones bring back memories
Of holidays by the sea.

I remember our sandcastle crumbling
As the tide crept up the beach
And white waves foaming and tumbling –
Where would the next one reach?

I remember peering in rockpools
And the cold, dark caves we explored
And looking down from the cliff-tops
Where the seagulls swung and soared.

Seashells and smooth, pink stones
All collected by me:
Memories on my window-sill.
Let's go back to the sea!

Eric Finney

48 Childhood

I used to think that grown-up people chose
To have stiff backs and wrinkles round their nose,
And veins like small fat snakes on either hand,
On purpose to be grand.
Till through the banisters I watched one day
My great-aunt Etty's friend who was going away,
And how her onyx beads had come unstrung.
I saw her grope to find them as they rolled;
And then I knew that she was helplessly old,
As I was helplessly young.

Frances Cornford (1886–1960)

49 Philip Fox

Pray, spare a thought for Philip Fox
Whose hobby was collecting rocks.
He'd still be here amongst us if
He hadn't done so on a cliff.

Colin West

50 Stone Circles

The ones
who set these stones
were shrewd, star-wise.

They knew the skies.

And plotted points
where sun and moon
would sink and rise.

They knew to measure,
calculate and place.

Transported massive weight
through tracts of space.

But why they hauled these stones
and set them so,
we only guess,
we cannot surely know.

Their thoughts, their reasons,
their intense belief
have blown away
on vanished winds,
light as a leaf.

The meaning's lost.
The flesh is gone.
All we have now are stones,
standing abandoned here
like remnant bones.

Tony Mitton

51 Taking a Chance

The chance to swim the Amazon
To climb up Kathmandu
The chance to ride white water
In a two-man crewed canoe
Such chances don't come every day
To meet your fear and face it
So, do not flinch or run away
But grasp it and embrace it …

Roger Stevens

52 Doubly my Ma

My Ma's love is a warm blanket
with the softest cosiest fleece.
I like to snuggle beside her
and shut tired eyes in peace.

Dida's love is doubly rich
because she is my Ma's Ma.
When she hugs and kisses me
I am a maharaja.

Debjani Chatterjee

53

Poet-trees

Whenever life's unkind to me,
I run off to hug a tree.
I find it helps when I am sad
and stops me going barking mad.

If I'm downcast, depressed and blue
my only comfort then, is yew.
I do my weeping under willows
it saves on handkerchiefs and pillows.

Who needs regression therapy?
I'm back to my roots with a tree.
If seas of troubles overwhelm
I can step up and take the elm.

As I get alder, it's plane to see
my elders taught so much to me.
Now, when I'm fed up to the teeth
I just turn over a new leaf.

Someday, I may pine away,
but I try to keep my fears at bay
and rest on laurels when life's good –
and that is quite a lot … Touch wood.

Jane Clarke

Sea-anemone

For such a tender face
A touch is like a danger.
But the dance of my many arms
To the music of the sea
Brings many a friend to me.

None can resist my grace.
All fall for my charms.

Many a friend, many a stranger,
Many an enemy
Melts in my embrace.
I am anemone.

Ted Hughes (1930–1998)

55 The Dog

The truth I do not stretch or shove
When I state the dog is full of love.
I've also proved, by actual test,
A wet dog is the lovingest.

Ogden Nash (1902–1971)

56 Algy Met a Bear

Algy met a bear,
A bear met Algy.
The bear was bulgy,
The bulge was Algy.

Anonymous

57 Good Morning, Mr Croco-doco-dile

Good morning, Mr Croco-doco-dile,
And how are you today?
I like to see you croco-smoco-smile
In your croco-woco-way.

From the tip of your beautiful croco-toco-tail
To your croco-hoco-head
You seem to me so croco-stoco-still
As if you're croco-doco-dead.

Perhaps if I touch your croco-cloco-claw
Or your croco-snoco-snout,
Or get up close to your croco-joco-jaw
I shall very soon find out.

But suddenly I croco-soco-see
In your croco-oco-eye
A curious kind of croco-gloco-gleam,
So I just don't think I'll try.

Forgive me, Mr Croco-doco-dile
But it's time I was away.
Let's talk a little croco-woco-while
Another croco-doco-day.

Charles Causley (1917–2003)

maggie and milly and molly and may

maggie and milly and molly and may
went down to the beach (to play one day)

and maggie discovered a shell that sang
so sweetly she forgot all her troubles, and

milly befriended a stranded star
whose rays five languid fingers were;

and molly was chased by a horrible thing
which raced sideways while blowing bubbles: and

may came home with a smooth round stone
as small as a world and as large as alone.

For whatever we lose (like a you or a me)
it's always ourselves we find in the sea

e e cummings (1894–1962)

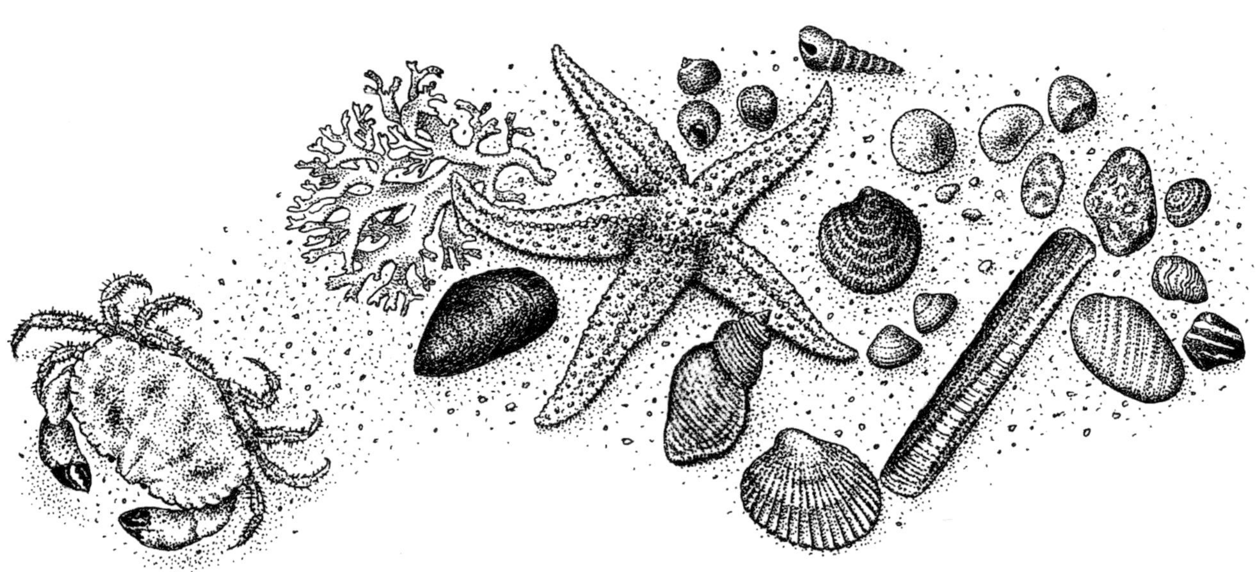

59 The Kiss

I found an autumn necklace in the hedge,
Silken threads, strung with tiny beads.
Yet when I touched a strand, it fell
Leaving only scattered tears.

I found a winter diamond on the wall,
Cold and sharp as a dragon's scale.
Yet though I locked it in a box
Somehow it stole itself away.

I found spring dancers in the wood,
Faces reaching for the sun.
Yet when I put them in a glass
Each grew heavy on its stem.

I found a summer moon beside the road,
Floating in a shallow pool.
Yet as I lifted it, it broke.
I cried; I'd meant to let it go.

Mum wrapped me in her strong warm arms,
Showed me the moon, still small and new.
"Some things," she said, "can't be owned,"
Then gave me a kiss, I have it still …

Sue Hardy-Dawson

60 The Discovery

There was an Indian, who had known no change,
Who strayed content along a sunlit beach
Gathering shells. He heard a sudden strange
Commingled noise; looked up; and gasped for speech.
For in the bay, where nothing was before,
Moved on the sea, by magic, huge canoes,
With bellying cloths on poles, and not one oar,
And fluttering coloured signs and clambering crews.

And he, in fear, this naked man alone,
His fallen hands forgetting all their shells,
His lips gone pale, knelt low behind a stone,
And stared, and saw, and did not understand,
Columbus's doom-burdened caravels
Slant to the shore, and all their seamen land.

J C Squire (1884–1958)

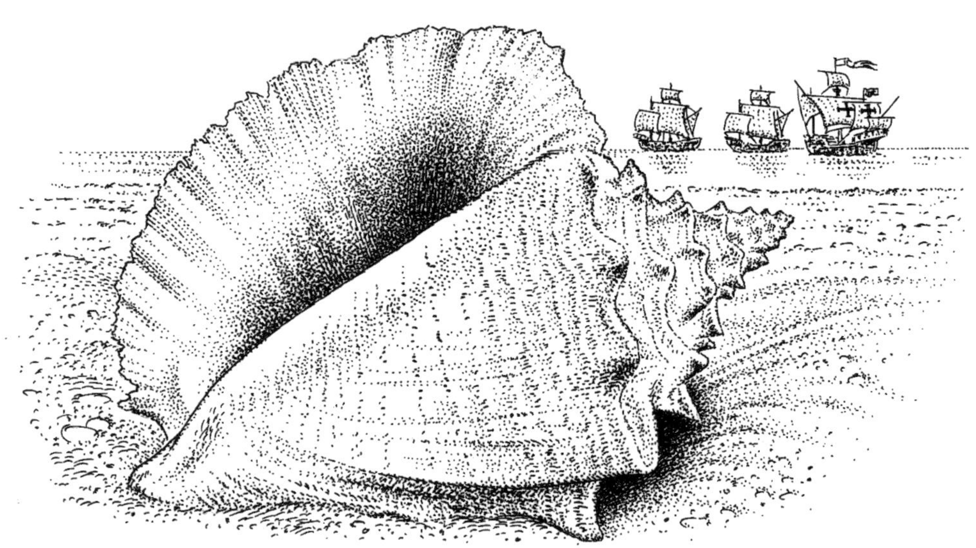

61 Dandelion Time

Dandelion
Clock tower.
No bell
To tell
The hour.

No tick,
No chime,
No face
To trace
The time.

No glass,
No sands.
Time blown,
Not shown
By hands.

Sue Cowling

The Loser

He lost his money first of all
And losing that is half the story –
And later on he tried a fall
With fate, in things less transitory
He lost his heart – and found it dead –
(His one and only true discovery),
And after that he lost his head,
And lost his chances of recovery.
He lost his honour bit by bit
Until the thing was out of question.
He worried so at losing it,
He lost his sleep and his digestion.
He lost his temper – and for good –
The remnants of his reputation,
His taste in wine, his choice of food,
And then, in rapid culmination,
His certitudes, his sense of truth,
His memory, his self control,
The love that graced his early youth,
And lastly his immortal soul.

Hilaire Belloc (1870–1953)

63 The Sorrow of Socks

Some socks are loners –
They can't live in pairs.
On washdays they've shown us
They want to be loners.
They puzzle their owners,
They hide in dark lairs.
Some socks are loners –
They won't live in pairs.

Wendy Cope

The Loser

With plaited mane and shining tack
We gleamed from top to toe,
My horse and I, in spirits high,
All ready for the Show!

For weeks I'd dreamt of winning cups,
Our pictures in the press!
To take away some ribbons gay,
A token of success.

Yet when we rode into the ring
Those hopes were fading fast,
The fences loomed and we were doomed,
I knew we would be last.

He flew the brush and knocked the gate
Before that awful wall,
Despite my stick and frantic kick
He wouldn't jump at all.

I turned him sharp to take him out,
We'd made a sorry sight –
And then he shied as he espied
The water glinting bright …

They pulled me out all dripping wet,
They set me on my horse,
Then all the crowd applauded loud
As if we'd cleared the course!

Cynthia Castellan

65 Lion

I have a box
in which I keep
a shoulder I may cry on,
I lift the lid
and there inside's
a large and lovely lion.

My lion is wild
with glorious mane,
a pounce in every paw,
I have to keep
him in a box
for fear that he may roar.

The box is small,
you'd hardly think
the King of Beasts would fit,
I only keep
my lion there
by training him to sit.

From time to time
I lift the lid
to hear my lion purr,
and gently stroke
my fingers through
his soft and friendly fur.

I have a box
in which I keep
a secret to rely on,
so carefully close
the lid upon
my large and lovely lion.

Celia Warren

66 Easter Monday

We tied the white eggs in onion skins,
wrapped them round with string.
We boiled them for so long
the water looked like strong tea.
Lifted out, the string was dirty khaki,
but the eggs – the eggs were glorious
marbled brown, amber and yellow.
When we were at the top of the hill,
when the others rolled theirs down to crack,
I held mine back –
it was too beautiful.

Catherine Benson

67 Reminiscence

The rain was ending, and light
Lifting the leaden skies.
It shone upon ceiling and floor
And dazzled a child's eyes.

Pale after fever, a captive
Apart from his schoolfellows,
He stood at the high room's window
With face to the pane pressed close,

And beheld an immense glory
Flooding with fire the drops
Spilled on miraculous leaves
Of the fresh green lime-tree tops.

Washed gravel glittered red
To a wall, and beyond it nine
Tall limes in the old inn-yard
Rose over the tall inn-sign.

And voices arose from beneath
Of boys from school set free,
Racing and chasing each other
With laughter and games and glee.

To the boy at the high room-window,
Gazing alone and apart,
There came a wish without reason,
A thought that shone through his heart.

I'll choose this moment and keep it,
He said to himself, for a vow,
To remember for ever and ever
As if it were always now.

Laurence Binyon (1869–1943)

68 Got you, Pirate!

"I'm a pirate bad and bold
And wicked as can be,
Tell me where you keep your gold
Or a dead man you will be."

"Down below in the deep dark hold
Under the deck trap door
You'll find a treasure chest of gold
By the ladder to the floor."

"Unlock the trap door to your hold.
I'm going down to see
And if you've lied about the gold
A dead man you will be."

"GOT YOU, pirate bad and bold
And brainless as can be!
When you went down my deep dark hold
You forgot I had the key!"

Cynthia Mitchell

69 These Old Shoes

These old shoes
have scuffs and stains.
They've trudged through snow
and pelting rains.

They've tramped their way
to school each dawn.
And now they're wrinkled,
lined and worn.

But these old shoes
have danced with glee.
They've clambered up
our Climbing Tree.

They may have cracks
and fraying laces.
But these old shoes
have won at races.

They're down at heel
with thinning soles.
But once these shoes
were scoring goals.

They've pushed at pedals,
trod the street.
They've tapped in time
to music's beat.

They've stood at bus-stops
for an age.
They've stamped in puddles
(and with rage).

And if I listed
all they'd done,
this poem would simply
run and run.

But though they once
were bright and neat,
and though they've stoutly
served my feet,

they're battered now
and much too tight,
and so it's time
to say goodnight.

Let's lift the lid
from off the bin
and gently, softly
drop them in.

Tony Mitton

70 Fishing for Compliments

I've been fishing for Compliments
with baited breath
in the river of life.
So far I've caught:
a "My, what a clever boy",
a "Hi, handsome",
a "What a man" and
a "You're really funny".

I did catch a Small Insult
but I threw it back.

Colin McNaughton

71 Where Go the Boats?

Dark brown is the river,
Golden is the sand.
It flows along for ever,
With trees on either hand.

Green leaves a-floating,
Castles of the foam,
Boats of mine a-boating –
Where will all come home?

On goes the river
And out past the mill,
Away down the valley,
Away down the hill.

Away down the river,
A hundred miles or more,
Other little children
Shall bring my boats ashore.

Robert Louis Stevenson (1850–1894)

72 Cargoes

Quinquireme of Nineveh from distant Ophir
Rowing home to haven in sunny Palestine,
With a cargo of ivory,
And apes and peacocks,
Sandalwood, cedarwood, and sweet white wine.

Stately Spanish galleon coming from the Isthmus,
Dipping through the Tropics by the palm-green shores,
With a cargo of diamonds,
Emeralds, amethysts,
Topazes, and cinnamon, and gold moidores.

Dirty British coaster with a salt-caked smoke stack
Butting through the Channel in the mad March days,
With a cargo of Tyne coal,
Road-rail, pig-lead,
Firewood, iron-ware and cheap tin trays.

John Masefield (1878–1967)

73 There was an Old Man in a Pew

There was an Old Man in a pew,
Whose waistcoat was spotted with blue;
    But he tore it in pieces
    To give to his nieces,
That cheerful Old Man in a pew.

Edward Lear (1812–1888)

74 The Note

In class he passed me a message.
Why he picked me, I couldn't guess.
He called me names – and teacher's pet –
and I admit I was upset
'cos nothing in the note was true.
I thought I'd show Miss Fortescue.

Then I heard about his mother
who'd died, with his older brother,
in an accident last July,
and I sort of understood why
he'd pick on me, with my nice home
and mum, when he is so alone.

So rather than tell tales on him,
making his life even more grim,
I'll have a word with him today
and see if there is any way
to be friends, help him out somehow.
I'll start by tearing this note up now.

Jill Townsend

75 Shirt

My shirt is a token and symbol,
more than a cover for sun and rain,
my shirt is a signal,
and a teller of souls.

I can take off my shirt and tear it,
and so make a ripping razzly noise,
and the people will say,
"Look at him tear his shirt."

I can keep my shirt on.
I can stick around and sing like a little bird
and look 'em all in the eye and never be fazed.
I can keep my shirt on.

Carl Sandburg (1878–1967)

76 Needle and Thread

Needle and thread, needle and thread,
Sew me a song to sing in my head.

Needle and thread, needle and thread,
Sew me a lyric to live when I'm dead.

Needle and thread, needle and thread,
Sew me a sampler of all I have said

But words I have spoken, unkind or untrue,
Let me unpick them and sew them anew.

Celia Warren

77 My Sock and an Old English Proverb

At eight in the morning
a hole in the toe
by eight in the evening
will massively grow.
If only I'd found
a few minutes to sew
at eight in the morning
that hole in the toe:

a stitch in time
saves nine!

Celia Warren

78 The Loom of Time

Man's life is laid in the loom of time
To a pattern he does not see
While the weavers and the shuttles fly
Till the dawn of eternity.

Some shuttles are filled with silver threads
And some with threads of gold
While often but the darker threads
Are all that they may hold.

But the weaver watches with skilful eye
Each shuttle fly to and fro
And sees the pattern so deftly wrought
As the loom moves sure and slow.

God surely planned the pattern
Each thread, the dark and fair
Is chosen by his master's skill
And placed in the web with care.

God only knows its beauty
And guides the shuttles which hold
The threads so unattractive
As well as the threads of gold.

Not till each loom is silent
And the shuttles cease to fly
Shall God reveal the pattern
And explain the reason why

The dark threads were as needful
In the weaver's skilful hand
As the threads of gold and silver
For the pattern which he planned.

Anonymous

A TIME TO SEW

79 Shirts for us Kids

We had no machine
  And no electricity.
It was by oil-lamp-light
  That Ivy's dexterity
Most showed itself.
  She sat near the window
Where she got more light
  Making shirts for us kids
And skirts for herself.

I watched as she drove
  The needle in and out,
  Raising it to shoulder height
  To pull the thread taut,
Then plunging down again
A gradually shortening gesture.
  She cut the cloth into shapes
Sewed them together.
  They were good skirts and shirts,
And we were proud of them.
  "Did your Aunty make this?"
  Neighbours would say. And "Yes"
  We answered. "Yes."

She did it all
Save one small thing:
Who licked the cotton?
Twirled it in his fingers?
Threaded the needle
With a steady hand
And a sharp eye?
  It was I.

Gerard Benson

80 My Father is a Werewolf

My father is a werewolf,
Right now he's busy moulting.
He leaves his hairs on stairs and chairs.
It's really quite revolting.
And if my friends make comments
(For some of them are faddy),
I tell them it's the cat or dog.
I never say it's daddy.

Kaye Umansky

81 Silver

Slowly, silently, now the moon
Walks the night in her silver shoon;
This way, and that, she peers, and sees
Silver fruit upon silver trees;
One by one the casements catch
Her beams beneath the silvery thatch;
Couched in his kennel, like a log,
With paws of silver sleeps the dog;
From their shadowy cote the white breasts peep
Of doves in a silver-feathered sleep;
A harvest mouse goes scampering by,
With silver claws, and silver eye;
And moveless fish in the water gleam,
By silver reeds in a silver stream.

Walter de la Mare (1873–1956)

82 The Ship

There was no song nor shout of joy
Nor beam of moon or sun,
When she came back from the voyage
Long ago begun;
But twilight on the waters
Was quiet and grey,
And she glided steady, steady and pensive,
Over the open bay.

Her sails were brown and ragged,
And her crew hollow-eyed,
But their silent lips spoke content
And their shoulders pride;
Though she had no captives on her deck,
And in her hold
There were no heaps of corn or timber
Or silks or gold.

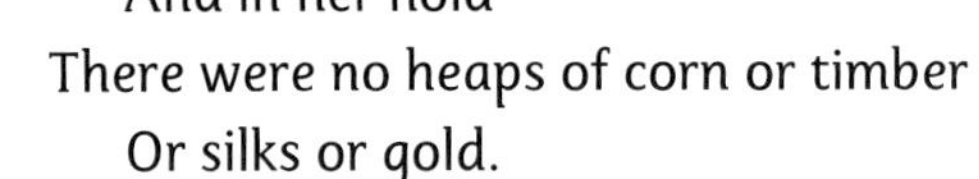

J C Squire (1884–1958)

83 Secret Love

"Oh tell me, tell me, Lizzie, please
Just what did Jason say.
I know he told you not to tell
But tell me anyway.
When he looks across the room
I go weak at the knees.
Do you think he's going to ask me out?
Oh tell me, Lizzie, please.
Did he say he liked me best?
Or does he like Louise?
Or is it Sue or Jane or Pam?
Oh tell me, Lizzie, please.
I've got to know what Jason said,
Oh, Liz don't be a tease.
I promise I won't say a word
Oh tell me, Lizzie, please."
"Well, can you keep a secret?"
Asked Lizzie, with a sigh.
"Of course I can," her friend replied,
And Liz said, "So can I!"

Gervase Phinn

84 Words

Words to whisper ...
Words to **SHOUT**.
To pack a punch!
To cast a doubt …
Words to relish
Words to chew.
ANTIQUE words
or words brand new.
Words to clacker and to clack
like trains that travel on a track.
Words to soothe, words to *sigh*
to shush and hush and lullaby.
Words to tickle or to tease
to murmur, hum or buzz like bees.
Words like hubbub, splash and splutter
wiffle, waffle, mumble, mutter.
Words that babble like a stream
Words to **SNAP**! when you feel mean.
Get lost! Drop dead! Take a hike!
Shut it! Beat it! On your bike!
Cruel words that taint and taunt.
Eerie words that howl and haunt.
Words with rhythm. Words with rhyme.
Words to make you feel just fine.
To clap your hands, tap your feet
or click your fingers to the beat.
Words to make you grow – or cower.
Have you heard the word?
WORDPOWER.

Michaela Morgan

85 A Conference of Cows

Here munching grass
Watching time pass

Chewing our cud
No thoughts of blood

Under us green
Above us blue

Welcome little words
like love and moo.

John Agard

86 The Bungalowner

I am a bungalowner,
I own a bungalow.
You'd never find a better home
No matter where you go.

We bungalowners never
Put on fancy airs,
And even if we drink too much
We don't fall down the stairs.

Everyone is equal,
That's what we always say.
We don't look down on anyone;
How could we anyway?

We've only got one storey;
For me just one will do.
I'll never rise to dizzy heights,
And never wanted to.

Come on you bungalowners!
Leave crowsnests to the crows;
So all together everyone:
I OWN A BUNGALOW!

Vernon Scannell (1922–2007)

87 Eighteenth Sonnet

Shall I compare thee to a summer's day?
Thou art more lovely and more temperate:
Rough winds do shake the darling buds of May,
And summer's lease hath all too short a date:
Sometime too hot the eye of heaven shines,
And often is his gold complexion dimmed;
And every fair from fair sometime declines,
By chance, or nature's changing course, untrimmed:
But thy eternal summer shall not fade,
Nor lose possession of that fair thou ow'st,
Nor shall death brag thou wander'st in his shade
When in eternal lines to time thou grow'st:
  So long as men can breathe or eyes can see,
  So long lives this, and this gives life to thee.

William Shakespeare (1564–1616)

88 Flowers

Some men never think of it.
You did. You'd come along
And say you'd nearly brought me flowers
But something had gone wrong.

The shop was closed. Or you had doubts –
The sort that minds like ours
Dream up incessantly. You thought
I might not want your flowers.

It made me smile and hug you then.
Now I can only smile.
But, look, the flowers you nearly brought
Have lasted all this while.

Wendy Cope

89 Haiku

Ah, the wretched man!
It's a thorny way I'll send him,
through my prickly hedge.

Matsuo Bashō (1644–1694)

90 The Sun has Burst the Sky

The sun has burst the sky
Because I love you
And the river its banks.

The sea laps the great rocks
Because I love you
And takes no heed of the moon dragging it away
And saying coldly "Constancy is not for you".

The blackbird fills the air
Because I love you
With spring and lawns and shadows falling on lawns.

The people walk in the street and laugh
I love you
And far down the river ships sound their hooters
Crazy with joy because I love you.

Jenny Joseph

from Auguries of Innocence

A robin redbreast in a cage
Puts all Heaven in a rage.

A dove-house filled with doves and pigeons
Shudders Hell through all its regions.

A dog starved at his master's gate
Predicts the ruin of the state.

A horse misused upon the road
Calls to Heaven for human blood.

Each outcry of the hunted hare
A fibre from the brain does tear.

A skylark wounded in the wing
A cherubim does cease to sing.

A game-cock clipped and armed for fight
Does the rising sun affright.

He who shall hurt the little wren
Shall never be beloved by men.

The wanton boy that kills the fly
Shall feel the spider's enmity.

William Blake (1757–1827)

92 Hate

My enemy came nigh;
And I
Stared fiercely in his face:
My lips went writhing back in a grimace,
And stern I watched him with a narrowed eye:

Then, as I turned away,
My enemy,
That bitter heart, and savage, said to me:

– Some day, when this is past;
When all the arrows that we have are cast;
We may ask one another why we hate,
And fail to find a story to relate:
It may seem to us, then, a mystery
That we could hate each other –
Thus said he; and did not turn away;
Waiting to hear what I might have to say!

But I fled quickly: fearing if I stayed,
I might have kissed him, as I would a maid.

James Stephens (1882–1950)

93 Whoo-ooo-ooo-ooooo!

Said the first ghost
On the old gate post,
"What I hate most
Is the co-o-old,
And being so o-o-old …
Five hundred years at least,
And being no use
To hen or goose,
Or man or beast.
And the wind in the trees
Which makes you freeze!"

"Whoo-ooo-ooo-ooooo!
What about you?"

Said the second ghost
On the old gate post,
"What I hate most
Is yoo-ooo-oouu,
When you suddenly say,
'Whoo-ooo-ooo-ooooo!'"

Gerard Benson

94 Evolution

I met my foe the other day;
we fought with fist and knee.
We grappled, shouldered,
kicked and roared
till finally, our limbs subdued,
each slunk away.

I met my foe the other day;
he came with fist
and I with sword.
I answered flesh
with sharpened steel,
he sank without a word.

I met my foe the other day;
I brought my dainty gun.
He bared his sword to greet me;
one finger crooked,
my foe was gone.

I saw my foe the other day –
no more than just a blur
across a smoky battlefield.
I saw him fall …
            or was it *her*?

I didn’t even see my foe –
no faces, no distress.
I pressed the button quickly
and found a wilderness.

Judith Nicholls

95 It isn't Right to Fight

You said, "It isn't right to fight."
But when we watched the news tonight,
You shook your fist and said
You wished the tyrant and his cronies dead.
When I asked why,
If it's not right to fight,
You gave a sigh.
You shook your head
And sadly said,
"Sometimes a cause is just
And, if there is no other way,
Perhaps you must."

John Foster

96 When a Knight Won his Spurs

When a knight won his spurs, in the stories of old,
He was gentle and brave, he was gallant and bold;
With a shield on his arm and a lance in his hand,
For God and for valour he rode through the land.

No charger have I, and no sword by my side,
Yet still to adventure and battle I ride,
Though back into storyland giants have fled,
And the knights are no more and the dragons are dead.

Let faith be my shield and let joy be my steed
'Gainst the dragons of anger, the ogres of greed;
And let me set free, with the sword of my youth,
From the castle of darkness, the power of the truth.

Jan Struther (1901–1953)

97 Nod

Softly along the road of evening,
In a twilight dim with rose,
Wrinkled with age, and drenched with dew,
Old Nod, the shepherd, goes.

His drowsy flock streams on before him,
Their fleeces charged with gold,
To where the sun's last beam leans low
On Nod the shepherd's fold.

The hedge is quick and green with briar,
From their sand the conies creep;
And all the birds that fly in heaven
Flock singing home to sleep.

His lambs outnumber a noon's roses,
Yet when night's shadows fall,
His blind old sheep-dog, Slumber-soon,
Misses not one of all.

His are the quiet steeps of dreamland,
The waters of no-more-pain,
His ram's bell rings 'neath an arch of stars,
"Rest, rest, and rest again."

Walter de la Mare (1873–1956)

98 Prayer for Peace

Lord, make me an instrument of Thy peace;
where there is hatred, let me sow love;
where there is injury, pardon;
where there is doubt, faith;
where there is despair, hope;
where there is darkness, light;
and where there is sadness, joy.

St Francis of Assisi (1182–1226)

99 Adlestrop

Yes. I remember Adlestrop –
The name, because one afternoon
Of heat the express-train drew up there
Unwontedly. It was late June.

The steam hissed. Someone cleared his throat.
No one left and no one came
On the bare platform. What I saw
Was Adlestrop – only the name

And willows, willow-herb, and grass,
And meadowsweet, and haycocks dry,
No whit less still and lonely fair
Than the high cloudlets in the sky.

And for that minute a blackbird sang
Close by, and round him, mistier,
Farther and farther, all the birds
Of Oxfordshire and Gloucestershire.

Edward Thomas (1878–1917)

100 The Tree and the Pool

"I don't want my leaves to drop," said the tree.
"I don't want to freeze," said the pool.
"I don't want to smile," said the sombre man.
"Or ever to cry," said the Fool.

"I don't want to open," said the bud,
"I don't want to end," said the night.
"I don't want to rise," said the neap-tide,
"Or ever to fall," said the kite.

They wished and they murmured and whispered,
They said that to change was a crime,
Then a voice from nowhere answered,
"You must do what I say," said Time.

Brian Patten

Acknowledgements

Schofield & Sims has made every effort to obtain permission to reproduce all copyright material contained in this anthology, and the permissions granted are listed below. Each poem makes an important contribution to the collection and the Company would like to thank all those copyright holders who have given their consent. If any copyright holder whose work appears in this book has not been contacted, the poet or his or her representatives should contact Schofield & Sims so that an agreement may be reached.

'A Time for Everything' (page **1**) is adapted from the King James Version of the Bible (Old Testament). **'Haiku'** by Celia Warren (page **2**), copyright © Celia Warren, was first published in *Christmas Poems*, edited by Fiona Waters (Macmillan Children's Books, 2006) and is reproduced here by kind permission of the poet. **'An Elephant is Born'** by Liz Brownlee (page **2**), copyright © Liz Brownlee, was first published in *Shouting at the Ocean*, edited by Graham Denton, Andrea Shavick and Roger Stevens (Hands Up Books, 2009) and is included here by kind permission of the poet. **'A Final Appointment'** by Eric Finney (page **4**), copyright © Eric Finney 1987, was first published in *Another Third Poetry Book*, edited by John Foster (Oxford University Press, 1987) and is reproduced here by kind permission of the poet. **'Plum'** by Tony Mitton (page **10**), copyright © Tony Mitton, was first published in the book of the same title (*Plum* by Tony Mitton, Barn Owl Books, 1998, 2010), and is reproduced here by permission of David Higham Associates Limited. **'Bulb'** by Alison Chisholm (page **11**), copyright © Alison Chisholm, was first published in *How to Turn your Teacher Purple*, edited by James Carter (A & C Black, 2011) and is reproduced here by kind permission of the poet. **'The Nymph Considers the Garden'** by Alison Brackenbury (page **12**), copyright © Alison Brackenbury 2009, was first published in the online magazine *The Bow-Wow Shop* (www.bowwowshop.org.uk) and is reproduced here by kind permission of the poet. **'The Ghosts of Weeds'** by Nick Toczek (page **13**) is copyright © Nick Toczek 2013 and is reproduced here by kind permission of the poet. **'Good Taste'** by Christopher Logue (page **14**) is copyright © Christopher Logue 1959, and is reproduced here by permission of David Godwin Associates. **'Lovely Mosquito'** by Doug MacLeod (page **15**), copyright © Doug MacLeod, was first published in *In the Garden of Badthings* (Viking Kestrel, 1982) and is reproduced here by kind permission of the poet. **'The Wind'** by James Stephens (page **15**) is copyright © James Stephens and is reproduced here by permission of The Society of Authors as the Literary Representative of the Estate of James Stephens. **'On Killing a Tree'** by Gieve Patel (page **16**) is copyright © Gieve Patel and is reproduced here by kind permission of the poet. **'Necklace'** by Chrissie Gittins (page **22**), copyright © Chrissie Gittins, was first published in *The Humpback's Wail* (Rabbit Hole Publications, 2010), and is reproduced here by kind permission of the poet. **'Demolition Worker'** by Stanley Cook (page **23**) is copyright © the Estate of Stanley Cook and is reprinted here by permission of his daughter, Sarah Matthews. **'The Spiders Cast their Spell'** by John Agard (page **24**), copyright © 1996 by John Agard, is reproduced by kind permission of John Agard c/o Caroline Sheldon Literary Agency Limited. **'Spinner'** by Alison Brackenbury (page **26**), copyright © Alison Brackenbury, was first published in *Christmas Roses and Other Poems* by Alison Brackenbury (Carcanet

Books Limited, 1988) and is reproduced here by permission of the publisher. **'Target'** by Rachel Rooney (page **27**), copyright © Rachel Rooney, was first published in *The Language of Cat* by Rachel Rooney (Frances Lincoln, 2011) and is reproduced here by kind permission of the publisher. **'The Trouble with Snowmen'** by Roger McGough (page **28**), copyright © Roger McGough, was first published in *Defying Gravity* (© Roger McGough 1992) and is printed by permission of United Agents (www.unitedagents.co.uk) and Peters Fraser and Dunlop (www.pfd.co.uk) on behalf of Roger McGough. **'What has Happened to Lulu?'** by Charles Causley (page **29**), copyright © Charles Causley, is from *I Had a Little Cat* by Charles Causley (Macmillan, 2009) and is reproduced by permission of David Higham Associates. **'The Wind's Prize'** by Andrea Shavick (page **30**) is copyright © Andrea Shavick and is reproduced here by kind permission of Wade & Doherty Literary Agency Limited. **'Samantha is Sobbing'** by Gareth Owen (page **31**) is copyright © Gareth Owen and is reproduced here by permission of the poet c/o Rogers, Coleridge & White Limited, 20 Powis Mews, London W11 1JN. **'Daddy Fell into the Pond'** by Alfred Noyes (page **32**) is reproduced by permission of The Society of Authors, as the Literary Representative of the Estate of Alfred Noyes. **'Mrs Reece Laughs'** by Martin Armstrong (page **33**) is reprinted by permission of PFD (www.pfd.co.uk) on behalf of the Estate of Martin Armstrong. **'Laugh and be Merry'** by John Masefield (page **34**) is reproduced by permission of The Society of Authors as the Literary Representative of the Estate of John Masefield. **'The Laughter Forecast'** by Sue Cowling (page **35**) is copyright © Sue Cowling 2001 and is reproduced here by kind permission of the poet. **'Pantomime Poem'** by Coral Rumble (page **36**), copyright © Coral Rumble, was first published in *The School Year Book*, edited by Brian Moses (Macmillan, 2001), and is reproduced here by kind permission of the poet. **'Creator'** by Jane A Russell (page **37**), copyright © Jane A Russell, was first published in the journal *Envoi* (Cinnamon Press, 1997) and is reproduced by kind permission of the poet. **'Dog End Days'** by Michaela Morgan (page **38**), copyright © Michaela Morgan, was first published in *The Works*, edited by Paul Cookson (Macmillan Children's Books, 2000) and is reproduced here with the kind permission of the poet. **'Stop All the Clocks'** by W H Auden (page **39**) is copyright © 1936, The Estate of W H Auden and is reproduced by permission of The Wylie Agency (UK) Limited. **'Tarantella'** by Hilaire Belloc (page **42**), copyright © Hilaire Belloc 1923, is from *Complete Verse* (Jonathan Cape, 1999) and is reprinted by permission of Peters Fraser and Dunlop (www.pfd.co.uk) on behalf of the Estate of Hilaire Belloc. **'The Ballet Teacher'** by Chrissie Gittins (page **43**), copyright © Chrissie Gittins, was first published in *I Don't Want an Avocado for an Uncle* (Rabbit Hole Publications, 2006) and is reproduced here by kind permission of the poet. **'In the Misty, Murky Graveyard'** by Wes Magee (page **44**), copyright © Wes Magee, was first published in *Unzip Your Lips* by Paul Cookson (Macmillan, 1998), and is reproduced here by kind permission of the poet. **'Stony'** by Eric Finney (page **46**), copyright © Eric Finney 1987, was first published in *Another First Poetry Book*, edited by John Foster (Oxford University Press, 1987) and is reproduced here by kind permission of the poet. **'Jacks'** by Jan Dean (page **47**), copyright © Jan Dean 2013, is reproduced here by kind permission of the poet. **'Shells and Stones'** by Eric Finney (page **49**) is copyright © Eric Finney 2011 and is reproduced here by kind permission of the poet. **'Childhood'** by Frances Cornford (page **50**) is copyright © Frances Cornford and is reproduced here by permission of the trustees of the Frances Crofts Cornford Will Trust. **'Philip Fox'** by Colin West (page **50**), copyright © Colin West, was first published in *The Weightlifter's Laughter* (Book Guild Publishing, 2011) and is reproduced here by kind permission of the poet. **'Stone Circles'** by Tony Mitton (page **51**), copyright © Tony Mitton, was first published in *Plum* by Tony Mitton

(Barn Owl Books, 1998, 2010), and is reproduced here by permission of David Higham Associates Limited. **'Taking a Chance'** by Roger Stevens (page **52**) is copyright © Roger Stevens and is published here by kind permission of the poet. **'Doubly my Ma'** by Debjani Chatterjee (page **52**), copyright © Debjani Chatterjee, was first published in *I Love My Mum*, edited by Gaby Morgan (Macmillan Children's Books, 2006), and is reprinted here by kind permission of the poet. **'Poet-trees'** by Jane Clarke (page **53**), copyright © Jane Clarke, was first published in *Shouting at the Ocean* (Hands Up Books, 2009) and is reproduced here by kind permission of the poet. **'Sea-anemone'** by Ted Hughes (page **54**), copyright © Ted Hughes, is from *The Mermaid's Purse* (also by Ted Hughes) and is reproduced here by permission of the publisher, Faber and Faber Limited. **'The Dog'** by Ogden Nash (page **55**), copyright © Ogden Nash, is from *Candy is Dandy: The Best of Ogden Nash* (André Deutsch, 1983) and is reproduced by kind permission of the publisher, Carlton Publishing Group. **'Good Morning, Mr Croco-doco-dile'** by Charles Causley (page **56**), copyright © Charles Causley, is from *I Had a Little Cat* by Charles Causley (Macmillan, 2009) and is published by permission of David Higham Associates Limited. **'maggie and milly and molly and may'** by e e cummings (page **57**) is copyright © 1956, 1984, 1991 by the Trustees for the E E Cummings Trust, from *Complete Poems: 1904–1962* by E E Cummings, edited by George J Firmage. Used by permission of Liveright Publishing Corporation. **'The Kiss'** by Sue Hardy-Dawson (page **58**) is copyright © Sue Hardy-Dawson 2013 and is published here by kind permission of the poet. **'The Discovery'** by J C Squire (page **59**) is copyright © J C Squire and is reproduced here by kind permission of Roger Squire, grandson of the poet. **'Dandelion Time'** by Sue Cowling (page **60**), copyright © Sue Cowling, is from *The Works: Every Kind of Poem You Will Ever Need for the Literacy Hour*, edited by Paul Cookson (Macmillan Children's Books, 2000/10) and is reproduced here by kind permission of the poet. **'The Loser'** by Hilaire Belloc (page **61**), copyright © Hilaire Belloc 1923, is from *Complete Verse* (Jonathan Cape, 1999) and is reprinted by permission of Peters Fraser and Dunlop (www.pfd.co.uk) on behalf of the Estate of Hilaire Belloc. **'The Sorrow of Socks'** by Wendy Cope (page **62**), copyright © Wendy Cope 2001, is from *If I Don't Know* (Faber and Faber, 2001) and is reprinted by permission of United Agents on behalf of Wendy Cope. **'The Loser'** by Cynthia Castellan (page **63**) was first published in *The Pony Annual*, edited by Genevieve Murphy (Purnell Books, Paulton, Bristol, 1983), and is reproduced here by kind permission of the poet. **'Lion'** by Celia Warren (page **64**), copyright © Celia Warren, was first published in *The Hippo Book of Magic Poems*, edited by Jennifer Curry (Scholastic, 1997), and is reproduced here by kind permission of the poet. **'Easter Monday'** by Catherine Benson (page **65**), copyright © Catherine Benson, was first published in *Frogs in Clogs*, edited by Gaby Morgan (Macmillan, 2005) and is reproduced by kind permission of the poet. **'Reminiscence'** by Laurence Binyon (page **66**), copyright © Laurence Binyon, is reproduced here by permission of The Society of Authors, as the Literary Representative of the Estate of Laurence Binyon. **'Got you, Pirate!'** by Cynthia Mitchell (page **67**), copyright © Cynthia Mitchell, was first published by the BBC in *Poetry Corner*, Autumn 1983, and is reproduced here by kind permission of the poet. **'These Old Shoes'** by Tony Mitton (page **68**), copyright © Tony Mitton, was first published in *Plum* by Tony Mitton (Barn Owl Books, 1998, 2010), and is reproduced here by permission of David Higham Associates Limited. **'Fishing for Compliments'** by Colin McNaughton (page **69**) is copyright © 1999 Colin McNaughton, and is from *Wish You Were Here (and I Wasn't)* by Colin McNaughton, reproduced by permission of Walker Books Limited, London SE11 5HJ (www.walker.co.uk). **'Cargoes'** by John Masefield (page **71**) is copyright © John Masefield and is reproduced here by kind permission of The Society of Authors as the Literary

Index of poets

Note for all readers

Please note that if a poet was no longer alive at the time when this edition of the anthology was first published, his or her dates of birth and death are provided at the end of the poem, beside the poet's name. If a poet was still alive at the time of publication, no such dates are provided.

Index of titles